The Ultimate Guide to Planning for Retirement

Crafting Your Personalized Retirement Plan: Navigating the Key Decisions for a Successful Future

Edwin B. Adams

Table of content

Introduction

Chapter 1:Knowing how to prepare for retirement

Chapter 2 :Evaluating your requirements for retirement

Options for saving for retirement

Chapter 3:Techniques for a Happy Retirement

Chapter 4:Making crucial choices for a successful retirement

Chapter 5:Recognizing and evading common mistakes in retirement planning

Introduction

Everybody aspires to reach the milestone of retirement. It signifies the conclusion of one's working life and the start of a new one. It's a time to unwind, explore interests, and spend time with those you care about. But if enough preparation is not done for retirement, this ideal could become a nightmare. It is now essential for people to plan and invest for their retirement due to rising life expectancy and rising living expenses.

The process of identifying your financial objectives and developing a plan to reach them is known as retirement planning. It entails putting aside enough cash to support your desired lifestyle and pay for living expenses after retirement. It also entails managing your money to save taxes and increase your retirement savings.

People must take charge of their retirement planning in the modern world due to the unpredictability of the economy and the lack of pension plans. Relying only on employer-sponsored pension plans or social security benefits is no longer sufficient. Rather, people should plan and manage their retirement funds proactively.

It is impossible to exaggerate the significance of retirement preparation. To achieve financial independence and security during your elder years, this is a crucial step. A well-thought-out retirement gives people the flexibility to spend their time and money in any way they like without worrying about running out of money.

The goal of this book is to offer a thorough approach to retirement preparation, including everything from financial planning to lifestyle and emotional issues. It is intended to assist people in creating retirement plans that are tailored to their specific requirements and objectives at any point in their careers, whether they are just starting or getting close to retirement.

Chapter 1:Knowing how to prepare for retirement

An important part of one's financial life is retirement planning. It entails making choices and acting in certain ways to guarantee a pleasant and secure financial future beyond one's working years. Regardless of age or financial status, everyone needs to comprehend the significance and complexities of retirement planning. We will explore the idea of retirement planning, its advantages, and doable actions one may take to prepare for a safe future in this extensive content.

Retirement Planning: What Is It?

The process of saving enough money to sustain oneself during one's retirement years is known as retirement planning. It entails estimating the amount of money required for retirement and figuring out how to invest and save it. Creating a plan to guarantee a consistent flow of income and controlling spending to preserve a desired quality of living in old age are further components of retirement planning.

Why is it Important to Plan for Retirement?

Although retirement may seem far off, it is important to begin making plans for it now. Retirement planning is crucial for the following reasons:

1. Longevity: Individuals are living longer than in the past. The average life expectancy has greatly improved due to advances in healthcare and technology. Therefore, to prevent financial difficulties in later years, planning for a longer retirement term is essential.

2. Social Security is insufficient: For many people, social security serves as their primary source of income in their later years. Social Security income, however, might not be enough to support a person's preferred lifestyle. To augment social security benefits, it is crucial to save and invest for retirement.

3. Inflation: Over time, inflation can reduce the buying value of money. As a result, prices for goods and services may rise, and people's retirement savings may lose value. By guaranteeing that savings funds maintain their growth and keep up with the increasing cost of living, adequate retirement planning can help mitigate the consequences of inflation.

4. Financial Independence: Having a retirement plan gives people a sense of independence and financial stability. It frees them from the financial burden of depending on their kids or other family members to enjoy their golden years.

How Should Retirement Plans Be Made?

Now that we know how important retirement planning is, let's look at some doable actions you can do to begin saving for a safe future:

1. Get started as soon as feasible: It is best to begin retirement planning as soon as possible. Early beginning gives you more time to invest and save, and compound interest can increase your funds.

2. Establish retirement goals: Calculating the amount of money required to live comfortably in retirement is the first stage in retirement planning. Consider things like inflation, healthcare expenditures, and way of life today. Establish attainable goals and review them from time to time to make

necessary adjustments for evolving conditions.

3. Assess existing financial status: Before developing a retirement plan, it is imperative to have a comprehensive grasp of one's present financial status. This entails evaluating debts, assets, expenses, and income. It can assist in locating places that require modifications or enhancements.

4. Save and Invest: The next stage is to regularly save and invest money after determining your retirement goals and evaluating your present financial situation. One way to do this is to put some of your income into an IRA or 401(k) retirement plan. To lower risks and possible losses, investment diversification is also crucial.

5. Consider expert assistance: Retirement planning can be complicated. Getting guidance from a financial advisor or retirement planner can assist people in developing a customized and successful retirement plan that takes into account their particular circumstances and aspirations.

Chapter 2 :Evaluating your requirements for retirement

It becomes more crucial to evaluate our retirement demands as we get closer to the end of our lives. It is important to understand your current financial status, your retirement aspirations, and your projected income needs, so retirement planning is not something to be taken lightly. We will examine each of these topics in-depth in this extensive content to assist you in determining your retirement needs.

A. Recognizing Your Present Financial Circumstance

Understanding your present financial status is the first step in determining your retirement needs. Taking stock of your possessions, finances, debts, and other revenue streams is part of this. Your retirement plans will be built based on a realistic assessment of your financial situation.

Making a budget is one approach to acquiring a better grasp of your financial situation. This can assist you in keeping tabs on your expenses and pinpointing potential areas fcr savings so that you may increase your retirement savings. To make sure your investments are in line with your retirement objectives, you should also analyze them and think about speaking with a financial counselor.

B. Determining Your Retirement Objectives

Since they are determined by lifestyle choices, personal preferences, and intended standard of living, retirement objectives are specific to each person. While some people may wish to explore the world, others may wish to follow their interests and hobbies or spend more time with their family.

Spend some time thinking about what you want out of your retirement years to determine your retirement goals. Write down your goals and the kind of life you want to lead. You may prepare for your retirement by estimating the cost of reaching your goals if you have a good grasp of them.

C. Estimating Your Requirements for Retirement Income

Finding your retirement income needs comes next, once you've assessed your existing financial status and determined your retirement objectives. This entails projecting how much income you'll require in retirement to meet your needs and preserve your preferred level of living.

Start by thinking about your monthly outlays for things like food, housing, and medical care. Remember to account for any unexpected costs that might occur in retirement, such as those related to hobbies or travel. Next, assess your retirement income options, including personal savings, pension programs, and Social Security. To augment your retirement income, you might also look into alternative possibilities like part-time employment or rental income.

It's crucial to take inflation into account and how it can affect your need for retirement income. It is crucial to account for inflation in your calculations since it has the potential to gradually reduce the value of your money. Seeking advice from a financial counselor might also be beneficial to determine your retirement income requirements more precisely.

To sum up, one of the most important steps in financial planning for your later years is determining your retirement needs. You may make wise decisions and build a strong retirement plan by being aware of your current financial status, figuring out your retirement goals, and estimating your retirement income needs. Don't wait to evaluate your retirement needs; start making plans for a safe and happy retirement now.

Options for saving for retirement

A. Conventional IRA and 401(k) Accounts:

The classic 401(k) and individual retirement account (IRA) are two of the most popular retirement savings alternatives. A pre-tax part of an employee's pay can be contributed to a 401(k), an employer-sponsored retirement plan. This lowers the employee's taxable income because the contributions are taken out of their paycheck before the application of taxes. 401(k) plans are made even more alluring by the possibility of employer matching, which allows them to match a portion of employee contributions.

401(k) plans and Individual Retirement Accounts (IRA) are comparable, except IRAs are not employer-sponsored. They are a person's retirement account, which can be opened at a mutual fund business, bank, or brokerage house. Compared to 401(k) plans, IRA contribution limits are smaller, but they also provide tax benefits and growth that is delayed.

The tax advantage is the primary advantage of regular 401(k) and IRA accounts. Pre-tax contributions are made, which lowers a person's taxable income and perhaps their tax bracket. These accounts also grow their gains tax-deferred, which means that an individual's tax bracket is often lower when they withdraw the money during retirement.

However, regular IRA and 401(k) accounts have several disadvantages as well. Apart from income taxes, early withdrawals made before the age of 59 ½ could incur a penalty of 10%. Once a person becomes 72, they must also take Required Minimum Distributions (RMDs) from these accounts, which could result in a larger tax payment.

B. IRAs and Roth 401(k) Accounts:

IRA and Roth 401(k) accounts are two more well-liked options for retirement savings.

Similar to conventional IRA and 401(k) plans, Roth IRAs have tax advantages. The primary distinction is that contributions are made after taxes, which means that an individual's taxable income is not decreased. Withdrawals made during retirement are therefore tax-free. Employers can match employee Roth contributions as well, but the matching funds are still taxable when the employee withdraws them.

When it comes to retirement, people who expect to be in a higher tax bracket tend to favor Roth accounts. Long-term tax benefits are substantial because there is no income tax due upon withdrawal. After all, taxes are paid in advance. It's a flexible alternative for people who don't need the money in retirement because they don't have any minimum payout requirements.

Not everyone is qualified to contribute to a Roth account, which is one of its limitations. Employers may choose to offer Roth 401(k) plans, and there are income limits for Roth IRAs. An individual might not be able to utilize this retirement savings option if their company does not offer a Roth 401(k).

C. Benefits from Social Security:

For many people, Social Security benefits are a major component of their retirement funds. A government program called Social Security gives elderly people a source of income. The age at which a person begins receiving benefits and their average lifetime earnings determine how much they will get in benefits.

An individual must have worked and paid Social Security taxes for a specific number of years, often ten, to be eligible for Social Security benefits. Although the amount of benefits received varies, in 2021 $1,543 will be the average monthly payout.

Social Security benefits should not be the only source of income for retirees, even though they provide many with a safety net. The program's long-term viability is a source of concern, and the benefits could not be sufficient to meet all retirement-related costs.

D. Alternatives for Retirement Savings:

There are more retirement savings choices available in addition to Social Security income and conventional and Roth 401(k) and IRA accounts. Among them are:

1. Health Savings Accounts (HSAs): designed exclusively for medical bills, HSAs are tax-advantaged savings accounts. Pre-tax contributions are accepted, and profits increase tax-free. Tax-free withdrawals are also available for approved medical costs. HSAs can be used as a savings option for retirement-related medical costs.

2. Annuities: Annuities are insurance products that offer a retirement income stream that is guaranteed. Annuities can be

bought by a person with a one-time payment or with installments over time. In retirement, annuities can provide security and comfort, but they also have costs and restrictions.

3. Real Estate: Investing in real estate, such as buying rental homes, can guarantee a consistent income throughout retirement. Ongoing management and a sizable initial investment are necessary for this strategy, though.

4. Individual Stocks, Bonds, and Mutual Funds: Investing in the stock market can be done through mutual funds, corporate bonds, or individual stocks. This carries a greater degree of risk even though it may yield larger possible returns. As retirement

draws near, it's critical to maintain a diverse portfolio and to examine and change assets regularly.

Chapter 3: Techniques for a Happy Retirement

Retirement is sometimes viewed as a significant turning point in life, a period for leisure, pastimes, and spending time with close friends and family. But having a successful retirement means being well-prepared and well-planned. Thanks to improvements in healthcare and increased life expectancies, retirees can now enjoy this stage of life for as long as twenty to thirty years or more. For this reason, having a strong strategy in place is essential to guaranteeing a relaxing and contented retirement. We'll talk about a few successful retirement ideas in this article.

1. Make early planning efforts:

Starting your retirement planning as soon as feasible is essential to success. Retirement is a far-off dream, but it's never too early to begin planning for it. You have more time to save and make changes to your financial plan the sooner you begin planning. Compound interest is another benefit of starting early that can help you save a lot more money over time.

2. Establish Your Retirement Objectives:

Establishing your retirement goals is the first stage in the retirement planning process. What goals do you have for the years you'll be retired? Which would you prefer: more family time, vacation, or taking up a new hobby? Establishing realistic goals will aid in the creation of a budget and retirement plan.

3. Establish a Budget for Retirement:

A good retirement requires budget creation. It assists you in calculating the amount of money you will require to support your retirement lifestyle. Think about all of your income sources, including savings, Social Security, and pensions. This can help you determine the amount of savings required to meet your retirement objectives.

4. Conserve Carefully:

Retirement savings is a long-term endeavor, and consistency in saving is essential to success. Try to set aside at least 10% to 15% of your monthly income for savings. You can afford to save a lower percentage of your income if you begin saving early. To meet your retirement objectives, you might need to save a higher percentage of your income if you begin later in life.

5. Make Smart Investments:

To reach your retirement objectives, you must invest your resources. To reduce risks, it is essential to diversify your investments and make intelligent financial decisions with your savings. To develop an investing strategy that fits both your retirement objectives and risk tolerance, speak with a financial advisor.

6. Pay Off Debts:

It is essential to settle any outstanding debts before retiring. Debts with high-interest rates might lower your income and deplete your retirement funds. Before retiring, make a strategy to pay off debts, including credit card bills.

7. Take Medical Expenses Into Account:

Expenses for healthcare often rise after retirement. Our healthcare needs tend to rise with age, so it's critical to account for these expenses while budgeting for retirement. To cover any future medical costs not covered by Medicare, think about getting long-term care insurance.

8. Maintain Your Health:

Maintaining your health not only helps you enjoy retirement more but also lowers your medical expenses. Make healthy lifestyle choices, consume a balanced diet, and exercise frequently to guarantee a high standard of living in retirement.

9. Consulting or Part-Time Work:

Retiring does not always mean completely giving up your job. Take into account opportunities for consultancy or part-time jobs to augment your income and maintain your mental and skill set. In retirement, this can also provide one with a feeling of purpose and contentment.

10. Adjust as needed and be adaptable:

Because life is unpredictable, you will need to be adaptable with your retirement strategy. Prepare to make changes and periodically review your retirement plan. This may entail selling your house or altering your investment portfolio.

Chapter 4:Making crucial choices for a successful retirement

A. Selecting an Appropriate Retirement Age

Since it denotes the end of one's working life and the start of a new one, the word "retirement" can be frightening to many people. But, if you prepare ahead of time and make the correct choices, this stage can also be full of opportunity and exciting possibilities. Deciding on the appropriate retirement age for yourself is one of the most significant decisions you will have to make before retiring.

While some people might know when they want to retire, others might have to make that decision depending on their personal preferences or financial circumstances. Making the greatest choice for your retirement success requires serious consideration of your options and a detailed assessment of their benefits and drawbacks.

The appropriate retirement age should be chosen after taking into account several variables, including one's current income, future financial objectives, state of health, and interests outside of work. For example, working past the conventional retirement age can increase your savings and your

Social Security income, but it also takes away from your free time. Conversely, early retirement may result in lower savings and Social Security benefits, but it will also free up more time for travel and leisure activities.

For assistance in determining the ideal retirement age for you, it is recommended that you speak with a financial advisor or retirement specialist who will consider your particular situation and objectives. Recall that your choice of retirement age will probably have a big influence on your level of financial security and contentment in retirement.

B. Timing Your Social Security Benefit Claim

For many retirees, Social Security payments are a vital source of income, and when you choose to claim your benefits can have a big impact on your retirement finances. Thus, choosing when to file for Social Security benefits is another crucial choice that will have a big impact on how successful your retirement will be.

Social Security benefits can be started as early as age 62, but the larger your benefit amount will be the later you file. Depending on your birth year, there are differences in the full retirement age—the age at which you can collect 100% of your Social Security pension. In general, for people born in 1943 or later, it is between 66 and 67 years old.

You might desire to start receiving Social Security payments early for a variety of reasons, such as a shortened life expectancy or the need to access income right away. Higher monthly benefits and a bigger total payout are available to you if you can postpone filing until you reach full retirement age or even later.

It's critical to thoroughly weigh your options and determine the possible consequences of claiming Social Security payments at various ages. To assist you in making a wise choice, you can also use internet resources or consult a financial planner.

C. Assessing the Costs and Options for Healthcare

A crucial component of retirement planning is assessing the expenses and available healthcare options. Your healthcare demands may increase as you get older, so it's important to have a plan in place to pay for possible bills.

Examining your existing health insurance plan and figuring out how it will change in retirement should be among your priorities. Will your employer's plan still cover you, or will you have to buy private coverage on your own? At age 65, you might also be eligible for Medicare; however, to make an informed choice, you must be aware of the various components and their associated expenses.

Furthermore, since Medicare does not cover all long-term care services, it might be prudent to think about long-term care insurance. The costs of services like assisted living facilities, nursing homes, and in-home care might be partially covered by this kind of insurance.

You can ensure that you are sufficiently covered for any future medical bills by assessing your healthcare alternatives and costs before retirement.

D. Organizing for Needs for Long-Term Care

Long-term care needs are not pleasant to think about, but they must be taken into account while making retirement plans. The U.S. Department of Health & Human

Services estimates that more than half of individuals who age 65 will at some point in their life need long-term care services.

If you don't prepare ahead, the cost of long-term care can quickly drain your resources and leave you vulnerable when you get older. Because of this, your total retirement plan must provide for long-term care needs.

As was previously noted, one way to aid with future costs is to acquire long-term care insurance. You can also look into other possibilities, including Medicaid or Medicare supplements, although there can be more eligibility requirements and restrictions with these.

It's never too early to begin thinking about and making plans for your future retirement and long-term care requirements. You'll safeguard your financial stability and enjoy a piece of mind going forward by doing this.

E. Handling Funds and Investing Techniques

A prosperous retirement depends on prudent money management. This covers managing debt, setting up a budget, and keeping an eye on your investments.

Making a retirement budget that details your anticipated spending and income sources should be one of your first actions. This might assist you in figuring out how much retirement savings you'll need and in adjusting your budget before you retire. Additionally, you must carefully manage your debt and strive to pay off any loans with high-interest rates before you retire.

Keeping an eye on your investment strategy is another essential component of sound financial management. It could make sense to make portfolio adjustments as you get closer to retirement to lower risk and guarantee a consistent flow of income.

Working with a financial advisor to create a sound financial plan that fits your risk tolerance and retirement objectives is always beneficial. They can also assist you in making the required changes as you approach retirement.

F. Keeping Up a Fit Lifestyle

Maintaining a healthy lifestyle is just as important as making financial retirement plans. Maintaining good physical and mental health is necessary to have a happy retirement and stay away from potentially expensive medical conditions.

As you get closer to retirement, you should prioritize keeping yourself physically well. This includes working out frequently, maintaining a healthy diet, and being aware of any health concerns.

Retirement is a time when mental wellness is equally vital. Retirement can be a big adjustment after years of employment and normal participation, which can cause feelings of loneliness and boredom. To retain a feeling of purpose and fulfillment after retirement, it's critical to continue participating in social activities, pursue interests and hobbies, and establish new objectives.

Chapter 5:Recognizing and evading common mistakes in retirement planning

A person's capacity to plan for retirement is crucial to their overall financial security and stability. On the other hand, it is not unusual for people to make mistakes when making retirement plans, which can have serious repercussions in their later years. Retirement planning blunders can range from small bumps in the road to major disasters, so people must recognize and steer clear of such hazards. Let's look at some typical blunders to avoid, how to bounce back from retirement planning setbacks, and how to stay safe from fraud and scams.

A. Typical Errors to Prevent

1. Procrastination: This is one of the biggest mistakes people make when planning for retirement. Many people delay retirement planning because they believe they have plenty of time. You will, however, be better off the earlier you begin retirement planning.

Solution: Make regular contributions to retirement funds beginning early in your working years. Compound interest allows even little contributions over longer periods to produce large consequences.

2. Not Having a Plan: Not having a retirement plan in place is another major error people make. Even while they might have some savings set aside for retirement, they risk depleting those funds too quickly or reaching their target retirement age before they have enough saved.

Solution: Create a retirement plan that accounts for your desired lifestyle, your anticipated retirement age, and any unforeseen expenses like medical bills.

3. Underestimating Expenses: A lot of people overestimate the amount they will get from their retirement savings while underestimating the expenses they will have in retirement. Making this error can result

in financial difficulties and living on a limited income in retirement.

Solution: Estimate your costs realistically and account for future inflation. When making retirement plans, take into account everything, including housing, healthcare, and recreational activities.

4. Not Diversifying Your Investments: Investing all of your retirement funds in a single class of securities is another error to avoid. Although this approach can appear secure, it could be hazardous if the investment underperforms.

The answer is to spread your investments throughout a variety of asset classes, including cash, bonds, stocks, and real estate. By using this strategy, you can reduce risks and possibly even enhance earnings.

5. Ignoring Taxes: When making retirement plans, a lot of people overlook taxes. Your retirement income can be greatly impacted by taxes, and unanticipated financial hardships can arise if you don't plan for them.

Solution: Speak with a financial counselor to learn about the tax consequences of your retirement accounts and think about ways to reduce your taxes, like making contributions to retirement accounts that are tax-advantaged.

B. How to Get Over Mistakes in Retirement Planning

1. Reevaluate Your Spending: Reevaluating your spending is the first thing to do if you've made a mistake in your retirement planning. Try cutting back on non-essential expenses or reducing your house as strategies to minimize costs.

2. Postpone Retirement: Try to postpone the age at which you will retire. You can save more for retirement and postpone taking withdrawals from your retirement funds by working a few more years.

3. Take into Account a Retirement Job: Working part-time during your retirement years is an additional choice. This can serve as a revenue booster and possibly cover any deficiency in savings.

4. Review investing plans: If your retirement accounts aren't generating enough income for you, you might need to review your investing plans. To create a new investing strategy and reevaluate your risk tolerance, think about speaking with a financial counselor.

C. Steer clear of fraud and scams when planning for retirement

1. Do Your Research and Verify: Be wary of claims that appear too good to be true when considering investing or seeking financial guidance. Before making any decisions, do your homework, double-check any facts, and speak with a reliable financial expert.

2. Beware of High-Pressure Sales Techniques: Salespeople who put you under pressure to buy a certain financial product should be avoided. Perhaps they're attempting to get you to invest in an inappropriate venture or fraud.

3. Be Wary of Guaranteed Returns: Investments with high return guarantees are sometimes a sign of impending fraud. Recall that bigger risks typically correspond with better profits.

4. Safeguard Personal Information: You should always exercise caution while disclosing financial and personal information. These details could be used by scammers to gain access to your retirement funds or steal your identity.

5. Remain Informed: Learn about typical fraud schemes and strategies utilized in retirement planning. Keep abreast with the most recent developments and news in the financial industry to identify any frauds.

To sum up, retirement planning is essential for ensuring the security and stability of finances during our golden years. We may guarantee a peaceful and worry-free retirement by avoiding frequent mistakes, being ready for accidents, and always being watchful against scams and fraud. It's never too late to begin retirement planning, and getting expert advice can help you avoid any potential traps. Recall that retirement is a period for unwinding and relishing the rewards of your efforts, so prepare carefully and steer clear of any needless pitfalls.

www.ingramcontent.com/pod-product-compliance
Lightning Source LLC
Chambersburg PA
CBHW071002290526
45795CB00005B/1748